LIFE ON A 1930s HOMESTEAD

HISTORICAL ARCHAEOLOGICAL INVESTIGATIONS OF THE BROWN HOMESTEAD ON THE MIDDLE AGUA FRIA RIVER, YAVAPAI COUNTY, ARIZONA

By

JAMES E. AYRES
GREGORY R. SEYMOUR

SWCA, INC.
Environmental Consultants
Flagstaff and Tucson, Arizona

SWCA ANTHROPOLOGICAL RESEARCH PAPER NUMBER 2

1993

Series editor: Robert C. Euler
Assistant editor: Richard V. N. Ahlstrom
Cover design and production: Christina Watkins
Copy editor: Sally P. Bennett

TABLE OF CONTENTS

LIST OF FIGURES

ACKNOWLEDGMENTS

As is usually the case in a historical archaeology project, people other than the archaeologists involved contributed in one way or another to this project. Even though many of these individuals were met only over the telephone, they were extremely generous with their time and knowledge and were tolerant of our prying into family affairs. Without their interest and unquestionably unique contributions, unavailable from any other source, very little could have been reported about the Brown homestead. These informants put the "meat on the bone" by personalizing what would have otherwise been a rather plain and ordinary site.

These helpful individuals were Jettie Brown Tyler North, Carroll Brown, Zona Oneta Avis Gilbreath, Bob Gilbreath, Doris Avis, Bobbie Murray, and Mrs. A. E. Burrell. Without the help of Mrs. A. E. Burrell, who led us to all the others, this would have been a very thin report indeed.

ABSTRACT

Charles J. Brown, a Phoenix home builder, was one of thousands of Arizonans whose life was unfavorably affected by the Great Depression. After he lost everything in Phoenix, Brown sought refuge from the rampant unemployment and economic stress of the time by selecting and homesteading 160 acres on the Agua Fria River in central Arizona northwest of Phoenix. He and his family lived on the homestead for about six years, from 1933 to 1939, surviving on money made from selling mesquite firewood, on gardening, on hunting and gathering, on goat, pig, and chicken raising, and on similar activities. The Brown family successfully survived the Depression on their homestead, eventually acquired a patent to the land, and later sold it to a local rancher.

The Brown homestead study provides a rare view of what a rural 1930s lifestyle was like on a not-atypical Arizona homestead. Insight into this existence was gained through three research topics, the Browns' subsistence and food-production behavior, sociocultural interaction, and vernacular architecture, among others. The sources of information that provided these insights were archaeological mapping and field observation, artifact collecting from the surface and from excavations, historical document research, and, most important, interviews of the Brown siblings. All were useful in demonstrating that the site is a significant historic resource.

INTRODUCTION

This research paper provides the results and evaluations of oral interviews, archival research, and archaeological investigations at the 1930s Brown homestead, AZ T:4:55(ASM). This testing program was conducted during July 1990 by SWCA, Inc., at the request of Jon Czaplicki of the Bureau of Reclamation (BOR). The work was authorized under BOR Task Order No. 7, Contract No. 9-CS-32-00600, and Delivery Order No. 9-PD-32-00600-007. This paper is a slightly revised version of SWCA's report to the Bureau of Reclamation on that project (Ayres and Seymour 1990).

The project area was adjacent to the Agua Fria River, some five miles northwest of New River, Arizona. Specifically, the site was located in T. 7N, R. 1E, Sec. 12, SW 1/4 and may be found on the USGS 7.5 minute New River, Arizona, Quadrangle (Figure 1).

During the spring of 1987, archaeologists from Dames and Moore, Inc., of Phoenix conducted a field reconnaissance of historic archaeological sites north of Lake Pleasant in Maricopa County, Arizona. Work completed under the Bureau of Reclamation's Plan 6 Historical Archaeological Studies Contract (Contract No. 6-CS-30-04360) provided an inventory and assessment of the historic archaeological sites that might be affected by the construction of the New Waddell Dam and the subsequent inundation of new flood zones. This supplemental survey resulted in identification of 15 historic sites (Ayres 1988), one of which was the Brown homestead.

The Brown homestead was considered to be a significant site eligible for the National Register of Historic Places under criterion "d" of 36 CFR part 60. The homestead was believed to have the potential to yield information on the nature of homesteading activities in general and about life on a homestead in central Arizona in particular (Ayres 1988:45).

Figure 1 locates the homesteads and ranches of the Brown family and their neighbors in the 1930s. The relationships between and among these parties are elaborated in some detail later in this paper, but a brief comment is necessary here to put each in the proper perspective. Charles and Ora Lee Brown had six children: Jettie, Oneta, JD, L.V., Carroll, and Mildred. Both Jettie and Oneta were married when Brown established his homestead, but only Jettie lived nearby. She was married to Albert Tyler and with him established the Tyler homestead west of the Browns' place. Later she married Ray Eulberg, and today she is married to Harry North. Oneta was married to Luther Burrell. The Browns' nearest neighbors were the Avis family, who lived less than half a mile to the northeast. Frank Avis and his wife, Doris, had two daughters, one of whom, Zona Oneta Avis Gilbreath, became an informant for this project. North of the Avis homestead were the residences of Art Prawl and a man referred to by the Avises as Tommy. The informants knew about these individuals, who, with the possible exception of Prawl, had had little impact on the Browns. Farther upstream was the Gingery ranch. C. A. Gingery despised homesteaders and seemingly did everything in his power to harass them. Finally, the homesteader who founded what is known today as the Little Grand Canyon Ranch, N. Bross Decker, appears to have had little impact on the Browns, although his homestead was at an important river crossing.

RESEARCH DESIGN

The research design for the Brown homestead was presented in its final form in a letter from Jon Czaplicki of the Bureau of Reclamation to R. Thomas Euler of SWCA, Inc., dated May 11, 1990. This letter identified three research topics suggested by James E. Ayres (1988:44) that could be addressed through investigation of the Brown homestead:

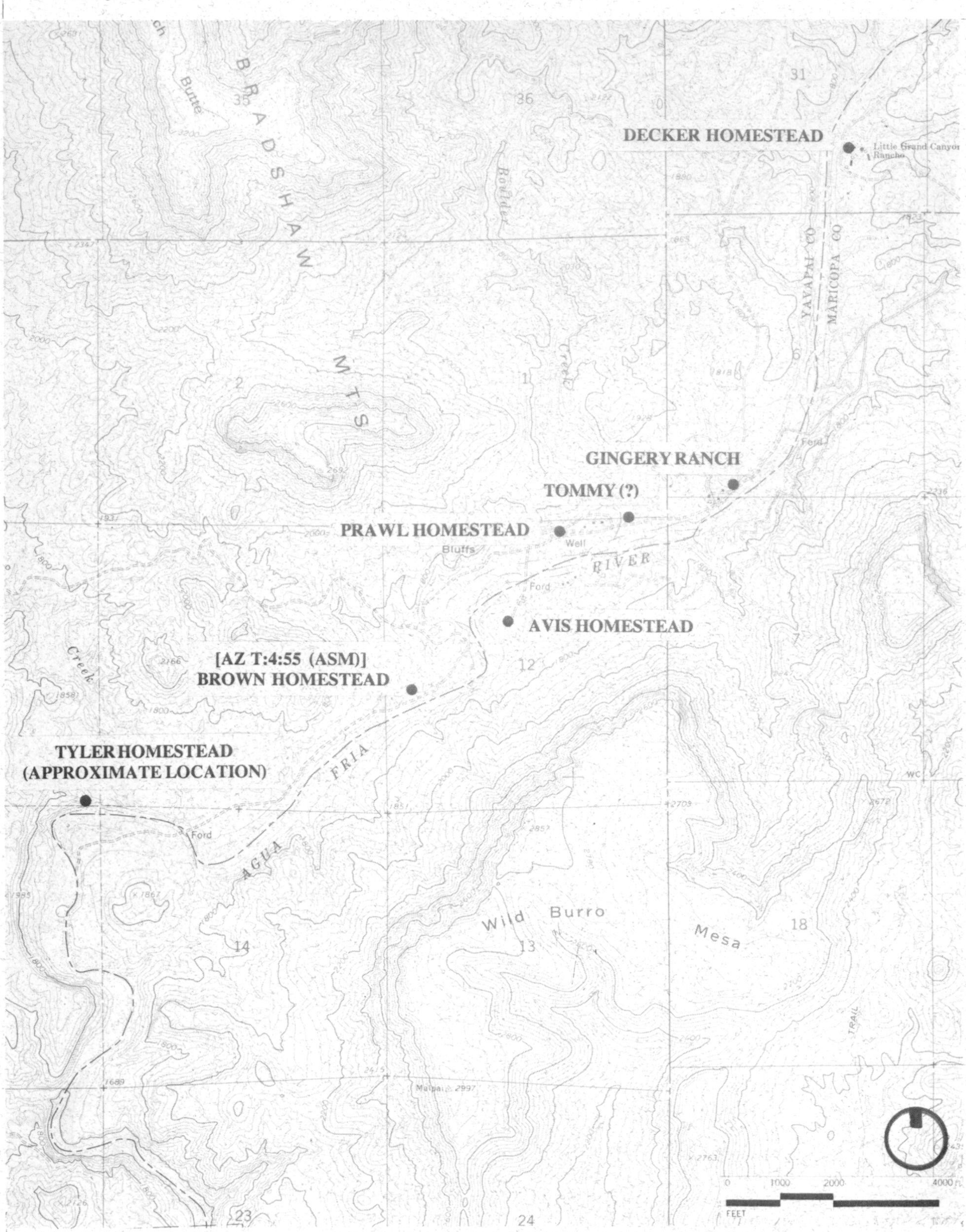

Figure 1. Location of the Brown homestead, AZ T:4:55 (ASM), and its neighbors. Base map copied from USGS 7.5 minute quadrangle, New River, Arizona.

The first research topic relates to subsistence and food behavior that can provide insights into the economic viability of homesteading and farming. Specific questions that can be addressed through analysis of subsistence data are: What was the role of purchased food versus home produced food? What was more important to successful homesteading, the amount of land cultivated or the ability to irrigate?

The second research topic focuses on sociocultural interaction between and among the site's occupants and both neighboring homesteads and the outside world. Sociocultural data will consist of information on visits between neighbors, parties, dances, labor exchanges, and contacts with the outside world through school, jobs, and church. Insights into some of the social problems affecting the homesteaders can be gleaned through information on feuds and disputes involving property, livestock, and fences. These data will be obtained primarily through oral interviews and legal documents.

The third research topic deals with vernacular architecture: the kinds of buildings erected on the site, their sizes and construction methods, the use of internal and external space, and the spatial relationship of the buildings to each other. These data can be used to assess the economic and social status of the homesteader, his attitudes about the expected length of occupation at a site, and how dwelling size may have been influenced by family size.

SOURCES AND INFORMANTS

Three sources provided information about the Brown family and its homesteading activities on the Agua Fria River in the 1930s: archaeology, historical records (including photographs), and informant interviews. All of these sources proved necessary to address the research topics discussed above.

The details of the archaeological effort are discussed elsewhere, but the other sources require some elaboration here. The major sources of documentary information were the homestead files and General Land Office (GLO) records and maps.

Ayres initially identified and documented the homestead through the files of the Arizona State Office of the Bureau of Land Management (BLM) in Phoenix. There he consulted the GLO cadastral survey maps for T. 7N, R. 1E and the 1937 surveyor's field notes for the map of that township, which was published in 1940. The records provided the patent numbers of the Brown and Tyler homesteads. Subsequently, he acquired copies of the relevant homestead records for both Brown and Tyler from the National Archives in Washington, D.C. The Tyler papers were useful because Tyler's wife had actually "proved up" that homestead by herself; as Brown's oldest daughter, she was closely connected to events at the Brown place. The homestead records consulted included the homestead entry forms, final proof forms, witnesses' statements, and the BLM's chronological list of actions relevant to the homestead.

The informants, those individuals possessing firsthand knowledge about the Brown homestead, were few in number. Brown took possession of his homestead in 1933, and the family moved from it for good more than half a century ago. The Tyler and Avis homesteads were also begun in 1930. All of the principals, that is the persons actually responsible for filing on the three homesteads mentioned, were deceased except for Doris Avis and Jettie Brown Tyler North. Doris Avis had been an invaluable informant during the 1987 survey of the area (Ayres 1988), but deteriorating health unfortunately prevented her from contributing much to the present study of the Brown homestead. A number of the children of all three families had been too young to recall much of the daily activities on the homesteads, and three of the Brown children were also deceased. Of the children, Carroll Brown proved extremely helpful and knowledgeable, while Jettie North, in her two roles as a homesteader in her own right and as a Brown daughter, was Ayres' only informant source for the Tyler homestead as well as an indispensable source of information about the Browns. Doris Avis, her daughter, Zona Oneta Avis Gilbreath, and Zona's husband, Bob Gilbreath, also assisted considerably.

The five informants provided most of the details presented below. Considering the years that have passed, it is not unexpected that the informants have forgotten, confused, or mixed up many details, or that they have compressed multiple events into one. Often the informants could not recall specific dates for events. Undoubtedly the way in which questions were asked or topics were pursued had an effect on what the informants recalled.

The interviews with Doris Avis, Zona Avis Gilbreath, Jettie Brown North, and Carroll Brown were conducted by telephone. Only Zona and Bob Gilbreath were visited in person. Although they had several photographs of the Avis homestead, they had none of the Brown homestead. Jettie North kindly lent the senior author six of her photographs of the Brown place, some of which appear in this paper. Data given by informants are followed in the text by their names in parentheses.

Although the Avises were known before this project began (Ayres 1988:24), no previous contact with the Brown family had been made. Locating the Brown family was no easy task. The Avises remembered most of the family but could not recall all of the first names, did not know where any of the Browns lived, and did not know the daughters' married names. They were able to recall the first names of five of the six children but not those of the parents. After discussing the problem with the Avises, researchers attempted to locate the Brown children using Phoenix area telephone directories and the homestead papers. The first approach was of no value but the latter indicated that some of the Brown family had lived in the Jerome and Clarkdale areas. Oneta Brown Burrell, who gave her address as Clarkdale in 1942, was one of Brown's daughters. As luck would have it, only one Burrell was listed in the local directory, having a Cottonwood address. This individual, Luther Burrell's second wife, was not related to the Browns in any way. Nevertheless, she directed Ayres to Oneta and Luther's daughter, Bobbie Murray, who was happy to provide the names and telephone numbers of the surviving Brown children, Jettie and Mildred in Chino Valley and Carroll in Delta, Colorado. Without the assistance of the elderly Mrs. Burrell, the Browns never would have been found.

ADDITIONAL INFORMATION

Jettie North, Ayres' principal informant, is variously referred to in this paper as Jettie Brown North, Jettie Brown Tyler, or even Jettie Brown Tyler North, depending on the time period involved and the circumstances being discussed. As another point of clarification, in some instances capital letters are used in the artifact description sections to indicate the presence of embossed brand name lettering or other markings on the artifacts. Generally, maker's marks are not treated in this manner but are simply referenced to the appropriate source, such as Toulouse (1971). Finally, there were not enough datable artifacts from any one feature to date it reliably, so dating was done only as a composite at the site level.

SITE DESCRIPTION

The Brown homestead was on an alluvial terrace on the northwest bank of the Agua Fria River, just east of Indian Mesa, at an elevation of about 1,680 feet. Vegetation on the site was primarily a mesquite woodland. Surrounding areas were representative of the Sonoran Desertscrub Community (Brown 1982). Features observed on the site included a house foundation, an adobe ruin, a privy, a dugout, a well, and a concrete tank. Artifactual material observed included evaporated milk cans, machine-made food cans, ceramics, glass, other metal, leather, shell, and hard rubber.

GENERAL FIELD METHODS

The brush was cleared from portions of the site to facilitate photographing, mapping, and excavation of the features. An arbitrary vertical datum was then established, and the site and surrounding topographic features were mapped. Artifacts, artifact concentrations, unusual or diagnostic artifacts, and visible surface features were pin flagged and then mapped. As is appropriate for a historic site, all measurements were made in feet and inches.

Next an artifact sample was collected from the surface of the site. Diagnostic artifacts were collected from each artifact concentration and from throughout the site. Large artifacts that were not collected were noted and recorded on the site map.

Hand excavation of five test units followed surface collection. Unit 1 in Feature 2 and Unit 3 in Feature 1 measured 30 × 36 inches, and the other three units measured 3 × 3 feet. Elevations were recorded in inches below site datum. Levels were excavated by cultural stratum when possible or by arbitrary 10-inch levels when not. All excavated soil was screened through 1/4-inch mesh, and all artifactual material was collected. Plan drawings of all excavated features were made, and all excavated areas were recorded using SWCA excavation forms. Black-and-white and color photographs provided an additional record of all subsurface excavations and of all features. The junior author, who served as field supervisor, kept a daily journal of all field activities.

HISTORY OF THE SITE

THE EARLY YEARS

Charles Judson Brown was born in Texas in 1883. He married in the early part of this century and supported his wife and family as a farmer. He and his wife, Ora Lee, began a family that ultimately included six children, the oldest of whom was Jettie, born in 1913. In 1916, shortly after the arrival of their second daughter, Oneta, the Browns moved to the Phoenix area of Arizona (Jettie North).

Brown's first attempt to provide a living for his family in Arizona involved the purchase of an ostrich farm in Glendale. However, because the national demand for ostrich feathers for women's hats and other accessories ended, the farm proved unsuccessful. Later Brown moved his family to Casa Grande, where he farmed for a while, and subsequently he worked as a carpenter in Jerome and at Fort Whipple in Prescott (Jettie North).

In the 1920s Brown and his brother took a correspondence course to learn, among other things, how to read architectural blueprints. About 1926 he worked as a carpenter on the construction of Waddell Dam, then known as the Frog Tanks Dam, and a year or so later he was working at Coolidge Dam. His family, which increased in size about every two years, moved with him from job to job (Jettie North).

Finally, in the late 1920s, armed with his carpentry experience and the knowledge acquired from the correspondence course, Brown began building tract housing in Phoenix. This business appears to have been very successful, but the success was short-lived. He had about 40 houses under construction when the crash of 1929 occurred. His home building/contracting business failed, he lost everything, and he owed several thousand dollars to building-material suppliers and others. Following the 1929 crash, Brown struggled to feed his family by operating a small fruit stand on Buckeye Road in Phoenix and at one time helped a local farmer irrigate his fields for 75 cents for a 12-hour shift (Jettie North).

Finally, unsuccessful in finding an adequate job in Phoenix, Brown saw an opportunity for acquiring a cheap place to live through homesteading and for making money by cutting and selling mesquite firewood from that land. After researching various potential areas open to homesteading, he selected the Agua Fria site in 1933.

Brown's homestead included 160 acres on both sides of the Agua Fria River in T. 7N R. 1E, Sec. 12, SW 1/4, roughly halfway between Indian and Wild Burro mesas. He constructed his house and other improvements in Sec 12, NW 1/4 SW 1/4, on the north side of the river. Actually, Brown simply "squatted" on the land in 1933 because, among other reasons, the land apparently had not been officially surveyed. He first filed a homestead entry form on the property in 1941 (two years after he had abandoned it) under the National Homestead Act of 1862, which among other things required that he reside on the land for five years and that he cultivate it.

During the Great Depression of the late 1920s and the 1930s, homesteading in Arizona became a popular way for many to maintain at least a subsistence way of life. During these years many Arizonans settled on the marginally productive, scattered parcels remaining open to homesteading. These lands could rarely support a family without some type of outside income. They often had inadequate water supplies, had little level, fertile ground on which to plant crops, and usually provided little or no forage for grazing animals. Commonly, homesteads of this period were located in extremely remote areas that were difficult to get to. In many cases, roads providing access were poor to nonexistent. Finally, many homesteaders were continuously harassed by ranchers who saw homesteaders acquiring for free the federal lands that the ranchers were often using illegally. Given all the obstacles, the number of homesteaders who were able to prove up their homesteads and obtain the patents to them is surprising.

BUILDING THE HOMESTEAD

According to his "Final Proof: Testimony of Claimant" form dated September 9, 1942, Brown moved to his homestead in October 1933 and camped out there with his son JD Melvin (the initials did not represent a name) until they built the first house. This was a simple one-room frame shed covered with sheets of corrugated metal. Brown purchased some building supplies in Phoenix, but he salvaged the lumber and sheet metal from an abandoned mine near Black Canyon City (Carroll Brown).

This building blew down during a violent storm and was washed away in the resultant flood. The second house, whose remains were located on the site (Features 2 and 4), had been a three-room frame and adobe building that Brown claimed to have constructed in 1933, although he probably had not done so until some time in 1934 (Carroll Brown).

The house, which was oriented northwest-southeast, consisted of three parts: a concrete-floored frame porch or entryway, a large frame room, and at the rear, a small adobe room. The porch was partially open on three sides with the entry in the center of the southeast side. At one time the northeast porch wall was covered. Four square timbers or posts situated along the southeast wall supported a sloping, tar-paper-covered roof. A low wall of river cobble and cement was constructed between and around the posts. The cobbles were built up around the posts about a foot higher than the segments between them (Figures 2 and 3). The large room, which had a wooden floor, served as a kitchen and as the parents' bedroom. It had a gable roof oriented southwest-northeast that was covered with tar paper. In addition to a bed, furnishings included a large kitchen range, in which the family burned mesquite and ironwood, and a large metal cabinet. Once when the family returned from being away, they discovered a skunk in the cabinet (Jettie North). The small adobe room that abutted the frame room served primarily as a bedroom for the children. It had a concrete floor, and the walls were covered with cement plaster hung on poultry netting (Carroll Brown; Jettie North). A wire-and-wood-post fence with ocotillo stems placed along it surrounded the house on at least three sides (Figure 2).

Brown had built the houses on a low terrace approximately 4 feet high on the west side of an unnamed wash draining the area north of the homestead into the Agua Fria River. Filling of the wash by sediments in recent years brought the bed of the wash up to the level of the terrace, resulting in periodic, probably annual, flooding of the site (Carroll Brown).

Brown and his son JD occupied the site to establish the homestead and to cut firewood to sell until the rest of the family joined them. At that time, there were six children, four girls and two boys, in the family. Jettie, the oldest, was married and soon lived on the Tyler homestead about a mile downstream. The other four children were Oneta, L.V. (Luiedell Victoria), Carroll, and Midge (Mildred). Two granddaughters, Jettie's daughter Alberta and Oneta's daughter Bobbie, also lived with the family part of the time (Figure 4).

A few months after Brown began his homestead activities in section 12, his son-in-law Albert J. Tyler and daughter Jettie established a 160-acre homestead about a mile downstream in T. 7N, R. 1E, sections 10, 14, and 15. Tyler filed his "Homestead Entry" form for his land on October 19, 1933,

Figure 2. View of the porch, Brown house. Charles J. Brown standing in front; part of frame room visible in the rear. Photo courtesy of Mrs. Jettie Brown North.

Figure 3. Porch detail, Brown house. Alberta Tyler, age 5, with the Brown family dog. Photo courtesy of Mrs. Jettie Brown North.

Figure 4. The Brown family at the Kay Copper Mine. In the rear L–R are Jettie, Charles, Ora Lee, Oneta, JD, and L. V. In the front L–R are Alberta Tyler, Mildred, Bobbie Burrell, and Carroll. Photo courtesy of Mrs. Jettie Brown North.

and later claimed that he established actual residency on March 10, 1934, according to his "Final Proof: Testimony of Claimant" form dated July 30, 1935. He claimed to have made all of his improvements in 1934. Tyler filed on his homestead under the same law as Brown, but because Tyler was a World War I veteran, he was allowed a veteran's preference that required the he reside on the property for only one year.

Albert and Jettie were married in 1929, and in 1931 they had a daughter, Alberta. They divorced in 1933, about the time Albert filed the homestead papers. Albert never actually resided on the property, but Jettie did with her daughter, and she proved up the homestead (Jettie North). Jettie maintained close ties to her family during this period and contributed materially and otherwise to their well-being.

After the Browns built their house, they had to dig a well. In fact, they dug three wells on the homestead (Carroll Brown). The first, located near the river, silted in and had to be abandoned. The second well was being excavated when the family mule died near the house. The mule had to be promptly disposed of, and the partially dug well was a logical grave site. The entire family was enlisted to drag the carcass to the well, where they buried it. The third, and final, well (Feature 9) was then excavated, probably to a depth of about 18 to 20 feet (Jettie North). A witness, son-in-law Luther Burrell, who was married to Brown's daughter Oneta, stated on his "Final Proof: Testimony of Witness" form dated September 9, 1942, that the well was 30 feet deep. A circular concrete water tank (Feature 8) was constructed on the west side of the well. Brown stated that the tank was 5 feet high and 16 feet in diameter and that it had been built in 1935. When measured by investigators, the tank proved to be 2 feet deep and 14 1/2 feet in diameter.

A windmill over the well had pumped water for irrigation and domestic uses. Although the wind had apparently been the primary source of power for pumping, Carroll Brown reported that the Browns had also used a gasoline engine to pump water and to operate a saw for cutting the firewood sold in Phoenix. The four wooden posts on the north side of the well depression appeared to have been part of an equipment mount where an engine had probably been placed. Also, Brown mentioned a "pumping plant" added in 1934 as an improvement. This item probably was the gasoline engine. Jettie did not recall that an engine had ever been used to pump water. In fact, it may not have been used often for that purpose.

The Delco light plant listed as one of Brown's improvements in 1935 provided electrical power. Ray Eulburg, who became Jettie's second husband, was responsible for bringing the plant to the homestead. The plant, situated near the house, never worked well and was too expensive for Brown to operate and maintain. Someone brought in an electrical refrigerator, but it too saw little use (Carroll Brown).

Near the river, the Browns built a corral for the goats, primarily using mesquite branches left over from the firewood cutting (Carroll Brown). Charles Brown gave no date for its construction, but Burrell listed the date as 1936 to 1937.

Finally, Brown listed "5 acres fenced with 6-wire fence" as an improvement built during 1934 to 1935, probably around the garden. Oneta Burrell stated that 5 acres were enclosed in 1935 with a 4-wire fence. Her husband reported that it was a 6-wire fence.

In general, Brown and his two witnesses agreed on most of the information about the number and types of improvements and on the dates they were added, but some discrepancies between their statements did occur. An area of major disagreement was in the value of the improvements listed (cost of materials plus labor). Brown listed his cost at $1,605.00, Luther Burrell estimated it as $1,285.00, and Oneta Burrell gave $780.00 as the figure. Oneta did not include the corral or the pumping plant. Luther Burrell also did not list the pumping plant. These figures represent an estimate, largely labor, with the cost of materials making up only a minimal portion. All in all, Oneta's figure probably most realistically reflected the real cost of the improvements.

Brown did not list as improvements two additional features at the site: the privy (Feature 1) and the dugout (Feature 6). The privy apparently had not been moved since its original construction, and the hole was only about 2 feet deep (Carroll Brown). The dugout in the terrace bank south of the house, intended for use as a root cellar and for general storage, was never completed, hence its absence from Brown's list of improvements (Carroll Brown).

SETTLING IN — LIFE ON THE HOMESTEAD

Achieving reliable access to the homestead was a constant problem. Good roads were virtually nonexistent, and a trip to Phoenix took most of a day. The Browns used two routes, one via Lake Pleasant and another more commonly traveled route that led directly from Phoenix north to the Table Mesa area, then west to a crossing of the Agua Fria River at Decker's homestead, now the Little Grand Canyon ranch (Ayres 1988:27). The riverbed could be driven most of the time, but during periods of high water this route was obviously closed. Also, the owner of the NO Ranch, C. A. Gingery, attempted to prevent the Avis family and one or two other homesteaders from having access to their property and shot Avis's livestock that trespassed on his property (Ayres 1988:26). Both Brown and Avis tried to find alternative routes into their homesteads to avoid Gingery, but they found it impractical and often impossible to avoid his property. Gingery's hatred of the homesteaders became so intense that on one occasion he and Frank Avis engaged in a fistfight. Avis severely injured one of his hands in this encounter (Carroll Brown; Zona Gilbreath). At this time, or perhaps at a later confrontation, Charles Brown was arrested, possibly for trespassing, and taken to Prescott. These events ended in a court battle that concluded with a judge awarding the homesteaders a right-of-way to their respective properties (Carroll Brown).

The homesteaders often became stuck in mud or sand or had their automobiles break down (Figure 5). Sometimes they would release some of the air from their tires to provide better traction in the sand (Jettie North). Once Jettie and one of her sisters had to walk to the homestead from Lake Pleasant, a distance of 8 to 10 miles, when their automobile broke down. On another occasion a Yavapai County tax assessor visited the Brown homestead to inventory their livestock and other property. He became stuck in the sand before he reached the homestead, and the Browns had to help him out of his predicament. Understandably, he declined to drive to the Tyler homestead, choosing instead to accept Jettie's word as to her holdings (Jettie North).

Part of the federal regulations governing homesteading included a requirement to cultivate the land. Although a practical stipulation in some regions, this almost absurd burden for those homesteaders settling in the Arizona desert nonetheless had to be complied with by all who homesteaded under the 1862 act. Despite undercapitalization, a lack of reliable water supplies, poor soil, and other factors, most homesteaders at least made a pretense of growing crops. They had to clear land, find water, plant crops and gardens, and protect their plantings from livestock and wildlife. Subsequently, on their final proof forms they made statements about the results that in many cases were untrue or exaggerated because few could raise crops successfully under the prevailing conditions.

Brown began the required cultivation process by clearing part of the mesquite bosque along the Agua Fria River that covered part of the north side of his 160 acres. This effort provided cash from the sale of wood and at the same time helped him comply with the federal regulations. He stated

Figure 5. Jettie Brown Tyler's automobile stuck in the Agua Fria River (a common predicament). Photo courtesy of Mrs. Jettie Brown North.

that by 1934 he had planted 3 acres of citrus, which had subsequently been destroyed by his goats, and 5 acres of vegetable garden. He said that the following year he had planted 15 acres of garden and wheat and that he continued this pattern through 1938. On land not cultivated, Brown grazed about 50 goats and several pigs. One of his sons believed that the citrus, which they watered by hand from the river, had never covered an area as great as 3 acres and that only a small plot of wheat had been test planted in one year, probably 1935 (Carroll Brown). Flooding also caused the demise of some of the citrus trees (Jettie North). It is unlikely that Brown ever actually cleared and planted 15 acres (Carroll Brown). Luther Burrell stated that Brown also planted barley from 1935 to 1938 and corn from 1936 to 1938, but Brown did not mention these crops. Burrell stated that the acreage was less than Brown claimed, totaling only 15 cleared and planted acres in 1937 and 1938. Oneta Burrell, Brown's other witness, reported that only 1 acre was cleared in 1934 as garden, only 5 acres were devoted to fruit, garden, and feed in 1935, and only 15 acres were planted in fruit, garden, and feed from 1936 to 1938. Apparently, the Department of Interior did not protest the discrepancies in the three statements, although they reflected an uncertainty as to the actual acreage and the crops involved.

The garden, which the Browns watered from the well, produced many regular garden items including tomatoes, peppers, green beans, corn, and squash, and also peanuts. Some of the garden produce, such as green beans, the Browns canned in fruit jars for later consumption (Jettie North). The goats constantly threatened the garden, indicating the need for a good fence to keep them out.

Brown also leased state land for grazing purposes. This undoubtedly exacerbated Gingery's dislike for homesteaders, because he had been able to use those same state lands for free. The Browns kept a number of different domesticated animals on the homestead over the years but consistently kept pigs and goats through most of their tenure on the site. Jettie remembered a mule, a burro, and chickens; in addition Carroll recalled two of three cows. The chicken house had been located under a big mesquite tree between the house (Features 2 and 4) and the dugout (Feature 6) in the side of the terrace (Carroll Brown). Jettie mentioned that she had acquired at least one pig, presumably for her homestead, from neighbor Frank Avis as a gift.

In general, the Browns allowed their goats and pigs to run loose to forage during the day and penned their livestock at night. Brown never purchased hay or other feed for his animals (Carroll Brown). The surrounding hilly areas provided a large grazing area, and the mesquite bosque produced enough mesquite beans to feed the pigs. Because the pigs' diet consisted almost entirely of beans, the cooked pork had a decidedly mesquite flavor (Jettie North).

The goats, pigs, and chickens provided meat for the family. In addition, the Browns drank goat's milk, used it in cooking, and occasionally made it into cheese (Jettie North). They also ate the eggs laid by the chickens. Meat that they could not consume within a couple of days or so after butchering was made into jerky or was smoked to keep it from spoiling because of the heat and lack of refrigeration. To make a smokehouse, Brown placed part of an abandoned automobile over the pit from which he had extracted the adobe to build the room on the house. The Browns burned mesquite chips for fuel and hung meat on the metal piece laid over the pit. Once Jettie smoked some river minnows to a golden brown, but no one wanted to eat them.

The family also tried to keep food cool with a "desert cooler," a small A-frame structure covered with burlap over which water was dripped (Jettie North; Carroll Brown). The food on shelves inside was kept cool by the evaporating water. Young cites a similar structure (in Stein 1988:83). Other than that it had been near the house, its exact location was unknown at the time of this investigation.

With money obtained from the sale of firewood, the Brown family purchased groceries in Phoenix including beans, flour, sugar, oatmeal, bacon, raisins, vinegar, and wheat. They toasted the wheat in the oven of the kitchen stove, ground it in a small mill, and ate it as cereal with goat's milk, sugar, and raisins (Jettie North). Charles Brown was something of a cook: he made a vinegar pie that all the children liked (Bobbie Murray).

Wild game also figured in the Browns' diet. Brown had two rifles, a .45-70 and a .22, and Jettie had a 410 shotgun that she and others used to shoot quail and cottontails. Once JD and Carroll shot a deer for food (Jettie North, Carroll Brown). On rare occasions JD and Carroll hiked the long distance to Lake Pleasant to try their luck at fishing (Carroll Brown).

Wild plant foods played a minor role in the Browns' diet. The family did make jelly made from prickly pear fruits, ate jojoba beans (and often put the beans in other food such as fudge), and also consumed mesquite beans.

The Brown family always had a limited amount of cash that was obtained from a variety of sources, primarily the sale of mesquite firewood cut and hauled to Phoenix in a large truck Brown had acquired. On at least one occasion the family sold pork at the Golden Belt and other mines in the Mayer area to obtain needed cash (Jettie North). The oldest son, JD, earned money by trapping coyotes, foxes, bobcats, ringtails, badgers, and raccoons and selling the furs in Phoenix (Carroll Brown). When he caught a bobcat, he could sell the meat to the Chinese in Phoenix (Jettie North). He also caught rattlesnakes and Gila monsters to sell to the Evans Reptile Garden in Phoenix. He received one dollar a piece for the snakes. Jettie said she also collected snakes and Gila monsters, which she kept in a steel barrel until she could sell them. Rattlesnakes were plentiful in the area; the first year the Browns lived on the homestead, they killed about 100 rattlesnakes (Carroll Brown; Jettie North).

Given the remote location, the family had difficulty providing an opportunity for the children to attend school. One year Jettie, the oldest daughter, obtained schoolbooks from Yavapai County and taught her siblings at home. Subsequently, Ora Lee and her children lived in a cabin at the Kay Copper Mine at Black Canyon City during the school session (Carroll Brown; Jettie North). The children also attended school in New River at one time (Carroll Brown). In 1936, when Ora Lee Brown left the homestead permanently moved to New River with the younger children (Jettie North). Similarly, one reason Jettie left her (Tyler) homestead after it was proved up in 1935 was to place her daughter into school (Jettie North).

The remoteness of the homestead and the condition of the roads prevented the family from having frequent contact with the outside, although the Browns often made trips to Phoenix. Much of the family's social contact was with a few neighbors, generally other homesteaders, and with prospectors, family, and friends. The Avis family, located on a homestead across the river and about half a mile to the southeast, and Art Prawl, who lived between the Browns and the NO Ranch, were the closest neighbors (Ayres 1988:24; Carroll Brown; Zona Gilbreath). Among regular visitors to the homestead were two or three prospectors who were working along the Agua Fria River. They occasionally stayed over night and, rarely, even for a few days (Jettie North). The family took visitors from the outside to see the prehistoric ruins at the top of Indian Mesa northwest of the homestead. The Brown children fully explored the ruins and petroglyphs that they frequently encountered in the area.

As was commonly the case in remote rural environments in the 1920s and 1930s, the need to provide subsistence required the effort of an entire family. There often was little time, money, or opportunity to entertain or engage in socializing away from one's immediate surroundings. Children usually entertained themselves in play and were often kept busy with a variety of chores. Outdoor activities predominated for homesteaders of all ages. The Agua Fria River had permanent but shallow surface water at both the Brown and Tyler homesteads. In addition to using this water for livestock, the families frequently played in it.

A windup Victrola-type phonograph player provided some music, and JD played the guitar. Homesteader Frank Avis's brother-in-law Jack also played a guitar, and on one or more occasions he played at the Browns' place while the others sang. This activity took place outdoors (Zona Gilbreath; Jettie North). Neighbor Art Prawl was also reported to be a guitar player (Carroll Brown).

Other recreational activities included attendance at dances in Black Canyon City or New River. The one-room schoolhouse in the former community, a popular dance place, saw frequent "wild times" (Jettie North). Jettie also reported that adults had frequently played poker, betting with Arizona tax tokens valued at one mill, or a tenth of a cent. They called the game "mill-ante poker," a play on "penny-ante poker" (Jettie North). One of these tokens was found in Feature 4, Unit 5. The youngest girls played paper dolls, and all the children enjoyed going barefoot (Bobbie Murray).

Christmas and birthdays were usually quiet affairs for the Browns, who had little money with which to buy presents, even for the children. Carroll recalled that for one Christmas his only gift had been a pocketknife given to him by neighbor Art Prawl.

In general, the surviving Brown children had good recollections of their homestead life. They frequently returned to the site to reminisce, to have a picnic, or to camp out. Jettie felt that life there had been a very positive experience and that homesteading under the circumstances had provided a good life for the children, even though the family had often been desperately poor during their homestead years, a very common state of affairs in Arizona during the years of the Great Depression. She thought that homesteading had been a physically taxing enterprise but that it also had been very rewarding. One of the advantages, she believed, was that through homesteading, one became close to, and even part of, nature. The rugged life had encouraged a level of Brown family togetherness and companionship that has survived half a century.

THE FINAL YEARS

Members of the Brown family occupied their homestead for nearly six years from late 1933 to September 1939, but the entire family did not live there together all of the time. After 1936, when Brown left with all of the younger children, only Charles and his son JD Melvin lived on the homestead, according to Brown's "Final Proof: Testimony of Claimant" form dated September 9, 1942, and to Jettie North.

By 1939 the Brown family was scattered. That year marked the end of the Great Depression and the beginning of better economic times and new job opportunities. Jettie and Oneta were married, Ora Lee and the younger children did not live on the homestead, and Charles Brown and JD moved to California. Jettie was living in California after her remarriage; in part, at least, this fact motivated Charles and JD to move to Brawley, California, where Charles found work in a defense-related industry. Thus, in 1939 the homestead was abandoned, never to be reoccupied by the Browns.

Although up to 1939 Brown was only a squatter because he had never filed formal homestead entry papers for his 160 acres, he did have correspondence with the Department of Interior's General Land Office about the property. Perhaps he could not file in 1933 because the area was unsurveyed (Jettie North). Whatever the reason, the General Land Office did not complete the survey of T. 7N, R. 1E until 1937 (Ayres 1988:22). The history of this aspect of the Brown homestead has remained unclear. As early as November 1933 Brown filed a notice of absence beginning on November 19, 1933, the length of which could not be determined. In effect, Brown was adhering to all of the regulations regarding homesteading under the National Homestead Act of 1862, but he did not or could not file the proper papers.

On November 21, 1938, Brown sent an affidavit to the land office correcting the legal description of his land to the SW 1/4 and protested any lease to anyone on the 160 acres involved. He claimed to have been a legitimate settler on the SW 1/4. Ayres could not ascertain what precipitated the affidavit. On September 8, 1939, Brown filed a notice of absence and a change of address to Brawley.

Perhaps recognizing the value of the land, or for other reasons, while he was in California, Brown proceeded to file the papers necessary to obtain a patent on the 160 acres. On September 2, 1941, he filed his "Homestead Entry" form Serial No. 073800 from Brawley. Ten days later he filed a notice terminating his absence, and on January 9, 1942, he submitted a change of address back to Arizona. A year after submitting his entry form he filed his "Final Proof: Testimony of Claimant" form dated September 9, 1942, along with the required "Final Proof: Testimony of Witness" forms from his daughter Oneta Burrell and her husband Luther. On his final proof form Brown listed his address as Jerome, Arizona. The Burrells lived in Clarkdale.

A slight hitch with the timing of the witnesses' statements did not appear to have held up the receipt of a patent (No. 1115272) for his 160 acres on November 11, 1942. Brown stated that he and the witnesses had not been present on the date set for final proof because he had not received the notice mailed to him. The land office retorted that the notice sent him had not been returned by the post office and, in fact, Brown and a banker had telephoned the land office and had been advised of the proof date.

Jettie thought that her father moved to Mayer, Arizona, upon his return from California in 1942 and later moved to Jerome, where he was living in September of that year. A year or so after receiving the patent to the 160-acre homestead, that is, about 1943 or 1944, Brown sold it to the Bard Cattle Company for approximately $2,200. At the same time Jettie sold the Tyler homestead (patented on June 15, 1937; No. 1090598) to Bard for $1,500.00 (Jettie North).

Investigators discovered little about the use of the property and buildings after Brown left. The buildings had been used by prospectors as occasional dwellings as late as the 1950s (Zona and Bob Gilbreath). There was no evidence that the Bard Cattle Company ever used the buildings.

Ora Lee and Charles were divorced sometime after she left the homestead. She subsequently remarried and continued to live in New River. In later years she and Charles were on good term; he often visited her and her new husband. Ora Lee died about 1976, and Charles, who never remarried, died in 1965 at the age of 82. All three are buried in the cemetery at Prescott, Arizona.

FEATURE DESCRIPTIONS AND EXCAVATION RESULTS

Ayres (1988) identified 10 features at the Brown homestead; the same numbering sequence was retained in the present study (Figure 6). With the exception of the privy (Feature 1), very little remained of the original buildings and structures at the homestead; therefore, many feature descriptions are necessarily brief. Following the feature descriptions is an identification of the artifacts from each feature with dates and other appropriate information. There were not enough datable artifacts from any one feature to provide reliable dates for each of them, so dating was done only at the site level.

FEATURE 1, EXCAVATION UNIT 3 (THE PRIVY)

Feature Description

Feature 1, the one-hole privy, was located in the northeastern corner of the site. It measured 40 inches in width, 60 inches in depth, and 72 inches in overall height and was primarily constructed of reused lumber and doors. Although the most intact building on the site, it was missing its door and part of the rear walls. A flat, oval piece of sheet steel, which may have been a roadside or business sign at one time, partially covered the roof. The automobile trunk lid found at the rear of the privy also may have been part of the roof cover. Framing consisted of 2 × 6-inch pieces in the front two corners, one on each side of the front edge of the seat, and probably in the rear two corners, although the latter were missing. The side walls from the doorway to the seat were covered with horizontally placed boards, 1 inch thick and 4 to 8 inches wide. The walls from the front of the seat to the rear wall were covered with pieces of paneled wooden doors. The material used to cover the real wall was unknown, but it probably had been either horizontally placed boards or doors.

The interior space between the doorway and the seat was approximately 28 inches deep and 36 inches wide. The seat area measured 32 inches in depth, 36 inches in width, and 16 inches in height. The seat was covered by 1 × 4- and 1 × 6-inch boards and framed by 2 × 2- and 2 × 4-inch boards. One of these framing pieces had half of a strap hinge on it. The single hole was set back 4 inches from the seat edge and measured 10 × 12 inches. It was framed by 2 × 4-inch boards.

The missing door had been attached by two strap hinges; the one on top was 5 inches in length, and the bottom hinge was 12 inches in length. Many sizes of common wire and finishing nails, ranging from 6d to 20d, had been used in the construction of the privy. Rocks were piled against the sides, possibly to fill or cover spaces between the ground surface and the privy. The sloping ground surface at the foot of the terrace had to be excavated to create a level space on which to set the privy. No other privy locations were observed on the site, but the movement of soil and rocks downslope on the terrace and the periodic flooding of the site had probably obscured any depressions that would have indicated earlier privy locations.

Excavation

A pit 30 × 36 inches was excavated on the interior of the privy under the area of the seat. Level 1 was an 11-inch-deep packrat midden. The midden material was removed and examined for historic artifacts, but no analyses of the plant and other material in the midden were made. Level 2, the first subsurface level, was 10 inches in depth and consisted of water-laid silt containing gravel and rocks. No evidence of a privy pit, staining, or other indications that the privy had been used were found during excavation. A shovel hole 12 inches in diameter was excavated to a depth of 17 inches

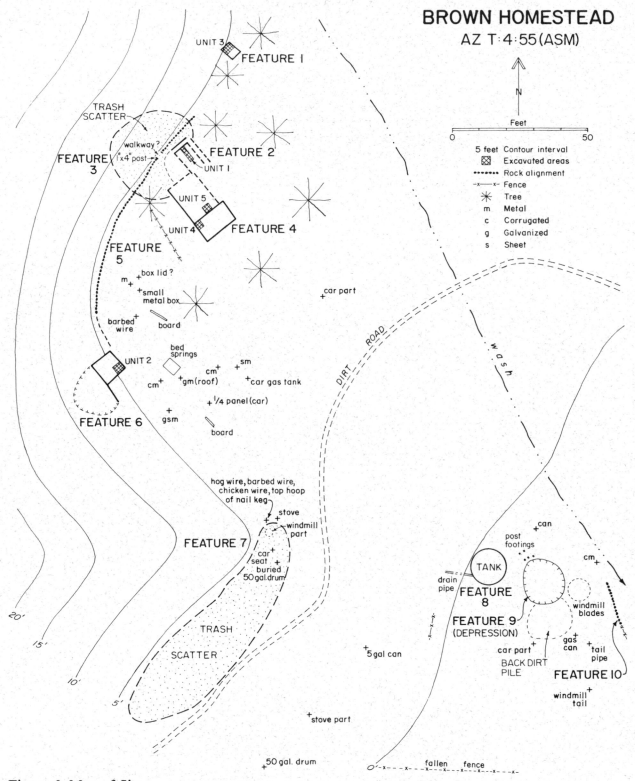

BROWN HOMESTEAD
AZ T:4:55(ASM)

N

Feet

0 ———————— 50

5 feet   Contour interval
⊠   Excavated areas
•••••••   Rock alignment
–x——x–   Fence
✳   Tree
m   Metal
c   Corrugated
g   Galvanized
s   Sheet

UNIT 3
FEATURE 1

TRASH
SCATTER
walkway?
1"x4" post
FEATURE
3
FEATURE 2
UNIT 1
UNIT 5
FEATURE 4
UNIT 4
FEATURE
5
m +   + box lid?
+ small
metal box
barbed +
wire   + board
bed
springs
UNIT 2
cm+   +sm
cm+   +gm(roof)   + car gas tank
+ ¼ panel(car)
FEATURE 6   +
gsm
board

hog wire, barbed wire,
chicken wire, top hoop
of nail keg
+ stove
+ windmill
part
FEATURE 7
car +
seat +
buried
50 gal. drum

TRASH
SCATTER

car part

DIRT   ROAD

w a s h

+ can
post
footings   + cm
TANK   +
drain   FEATURE
pipe   8
FEATURE 9   windmill
(DEPRESSION)   blades
car part   + gas   + tail
BACK DIRT   can   pipe
PILE   FEATURE 10
windmill +
tail

+ 5 gal can

20'

15'

10'

5'

+ stove part

+ 50 gal. drum

O –x – – x – –   fallen   fence – – x – – x –

Figure 6. Map of Site.

below the bottom of Level 2. The fill in this hole, labeled Level 3, resembled that in Level 2. Except for the first inch of Level 2, the fill was sterile.

Artifacts

Feature 1 artifacts came from the packrat midden (Level 1), which was heaped above the original ground surface on top of the area where the privy hole normally would have been. The artifacts in Level 2 were from the first inch of that level. No artifacts were found in Level 3. Found in the packrat midden were four fragments of leather, a piece of a woman's or girl's leather belt with an iron buckle attached, a piece of a man's leather shoe, a piece of a child's shoe, and another piece of leather belonging to one of the two shoes. Below the midden in Level 2 were five pieces of a man's work boot.

The automobile trunk lid found at the rear of the privy was not collected.

Faunal Analysis

Level 1 (the packrat nest) in Excavation Unit 3 produced a recent raccoon humerus (*Procyon lotor*), an artiodactyl humerus, and a long-bone fragment (Strand 1990). The two latter bones had been sawn and probably represented the remains of goats known to have been kept by the Brown family.

FEATURE 2, EXCAVATION UNIT 1 (HOUSE: ADOBE ROOM)

Feature Description

This feature was the remnant of a small adobe-brick room that had once been part of the Brown house. The room, 7 1/2 feet wide and 12 feet long, was open on the east side where it abutted against the frame room of Feature 4. Although not recognized as such during the survey, Features 2 and 4 were part of a single dwelling. The room walls had melted to a height of about 2 feet above the ground surface and were overlaid with the collapsed plaster-covered poultry netting (chicken wire) that had once been attached to the interior walls with 16d and 20d common wire nails. Imprinting on the interior of the plaster suggested that the adobe bricks had been about 4 × 10 × 18 inches in size. An uneven concrete floor using locally procured sand and gravel for aggregate had been poured on the interior of the building. One 2 × 4-inch board and a piece of corrugated sheet metal were partially buried in the adobe melt, suggesting that these had originally been part of the roof structure.

Excavation

Excavation Unit 1, placed in the northwest corner of the room, measured 1 1/2 × 6 feet and was excavated to a depth of 8 3/4 inches, where the concrete slab was encountered. Numerous artifacts were recovered from the fill, which consisted entirely of melted adobe.

Artifacts

Sixty-six artifacts were recovered from Excavation Unit 1, representing a minimum of 28 separate artifacts: 6 glass, 13 metal, and 9 objects made of other materials. No surface artifacts were present. The glass artifacts included a tumbler, an automobile headlight lens, a bottle, and clear glass fragments from 3 unidentified objects, probably bottles. The headlight lens was 9 3/4 inches in diameter and was flat with a ribbed pattern. The bottle was a square, 1 1/2-ounce machine-made container whose original contents were unknown. It had been made by the Owens-Illinois Glass Company in 1936 (Toulouse 1971:304).

Metal artifacts from this feature consisted of a small juice can, a tray, a piece of window screen, a shotgun shell, a belt buckle, a hacksaw blade, a crown cap, a safety pin, a piece of aluminum foil probably used as a cigarette or other product package liner, and four pieces of unidentifiable iron or steel. The juice can measured 202 by 214 (a standard manufacturer's measurement equal to 2 2/16 × 2 14/16 inches) and was opened repeatedly on both ends with a "church key" opener, presumably after the contents had been removed. This opener was first introduced in 1935. The metal tray measured 6 1/4 inches by 14 1/2 inches; it may have been a piece of kitchen furniture such as a cabinet, stove, or refrigerator. The 12-gauge shotgun shell had a "PETERS/VICTOR" headstamp dating to 1887 to 1934 (Hull-Walski and Ayres 1989:157).

Feature 2 produced nine artifacts, including a fruit pit, that were of materials other than glass or metal: fragments of roofing paper or a composition shingle, a plastic piece that separates powder and shot in a shotgun shell, a phonograph record, a small child's shoe, and otherwise unidentifiable fragments of rubber (two), hard rubber (two), and wood (one). The plastic piece, which had "Patented REM-PET" on it, dated to 1934 to 1960 and probably postdated the occupation of the homestead (Hull-Walski and Ayres 1989:154).

Faunal Analysis

Level 1 of Excavation Unit 1 produced three pieces of faunal material: a beef rib *(Bos* sp.), one bone fragment unidentifiable beyond the level of "large mammal," and one bone fragment unidentifiable at any level (Strand 1990). The rib and the large mammal fragment had been sawn. It seemed likely that both had come from a butchered domestic beef animal.

FEATURE 3 (TRASH SCATTER)

Feature Description

Feature 3 consisted of a moderate scatter of fragmentary glass, ceramics, and cans. These artifacts were spread from the north end of Feature 2 up the slope across Feature 5. The scatter measured approximately 30 feet in diameter.

Artifacts

The surface of Feature 3 produced 48 fragments representing 42 individual artifacts. These included 24 glass, 10 ceramic, and 8 metal objects. Various glass artifacts once contained food products: eight jars, two possible syrup jugs, and a bottle, all machine-made. Two "TABLE PRODUCTS, Co./LOS ANGELES" jars exhibited datable marks, indicating that one had been made by the Latchford-Marble Glass Company, 1939 to 1957, and one by the Glass Container Corporation, 1933 to 1956 (Toulouse 1971:332, 220). Three food jars had been manufactured by the Hazel-Atlas Glass Company, 1920 to 1964 (Toulouse 1971:239). The glass bottle once contained one of many Schilling's spices, or a similar product, and had been manufactured between 1918 and the present (Zumwalt 1980:366). Glass artifacts relating to leisure and recreational activities included a beer bottle, a dry snuff jar, and two pint wine bottles. All were machine made, and none had identifiable maker's marks. Investigators also found a tumbler for table use. Three machine-made bottles, the contents of which remained unknown, produced two maker's marks, one of the Maywood Glass Company, 1930 to 1961, and one of the Owens-Illinois Glass Company, 1936 (Toulouse 1971:357, 403). Five additional glass containers were represented only by a fragment each.

Ceramic artifacts were limited to nine tableware forms and one electrical insulator. In the former category were a dinner plate, two soup plates, two saucers, two bowls, and two unidentifiable forms. All except one of the soup plates exhibited some type of decoration, but no two had the same pattern of decoration. The plain soup plate and a saucer were porcelain; the rest were hardpaste white earthenware. The insulator was made by Porcelain Products, Inc., between 1927 and 1958 (Lehner 1988:586).

The eight metal artifacts collected were an evaporated milk can, a teaspoon, an oval tobacco can, a tin-can "patch," a cast-iron stove part, and three unidentifiable pieces of iron or steel. The milk can measured 214 by 315 and had a matchstick filler hole. The teaspoon had "SAXON SILVER PLATE" stamped on the reverse side of its handle. Dates for the can and the spoon could not be established. The tobacco can dates after about 1908. The patch, a flattened piece of a tin can about 2 1/4 × 3 inches in size with fine, small nail holes through it, had undoubtedly been used to patch or cover a hole.

Observed on the surface but not collected during the 1987 survey and not located in 1990 were a Karo syrup bottle, a Mason fruit jar, and a piece of ceramic tableware marked "ELPCO/MADE IN U.S.A." The latter dates to ca. 1925 to 1933 (Gates and Ormerod 1982:45).

FEATURE 4, EXCAVATION UNITS 4 AND 5 (HOUSE: FRAME ROOM AND PORCH)

Feature Description

This feature consisted of a concrete slab surrounded by a sandy concrete and cobble wall foundation, a dry-laid cobble alignment, numerous pieces of 1-inch lumber, 4 × 4-inch timbers, corrugated sheet metal, and other debris. Along with Feature 2, Feature 4 represented the remains of the Brown house (Figure 7). The concrete slab measured 7 × 13 feet and had been the floor for the southeast-facing porch. The foundation around the slab was made of river cobbles and cement. Different cement and sand mixes and a seam between the wall foundation and the slab suggested that the two had been constructed separately or at least had been poured using different batches of concrete.

A doorway approximately in the center of the southeast wall had an 8 × 8-inch concrete pillar on each side of it. Embedded in the middle of each pillar was a 4 × 4-inch wooden post. Lying on the southeast side of the slab were several 2 × 4-inch, 2 × 6-inch, and 4 × 4-inch pieces thought to have been part of the wall. These were later discovered to have been part of the porch roof (see Figures 2 and 3). On the northeast corner of the slab was a low concrete step to the doorway into the frame room. The step was 7 inches high, 13 1/2 inches deep, and 39 1/2 inches long.

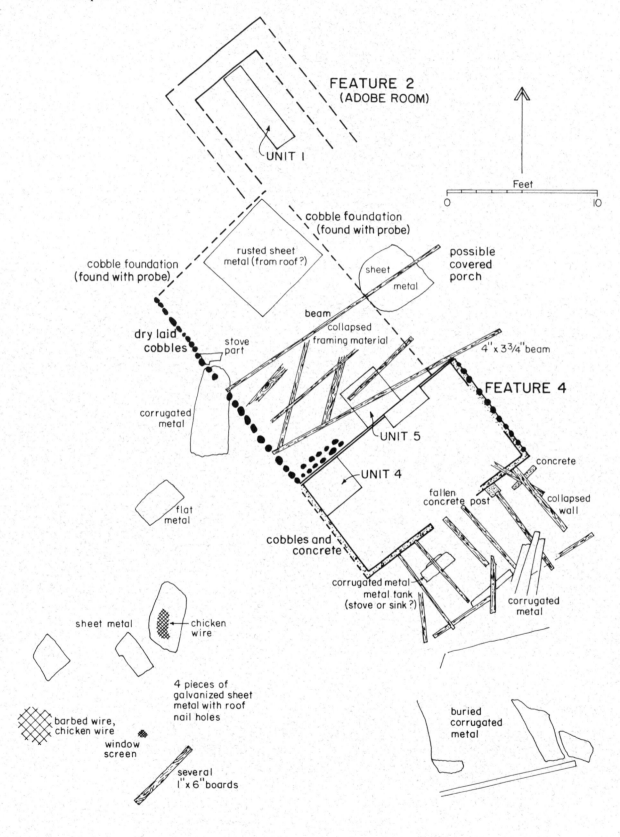

FEATURE 2
(ADOBE ROOM)

UNIT 1

Feet

0   10

cobble foundation
(found with probe)

cobble foundation
(found with probe)

rusted sheet
metal (from roof?)

possible
covered
porch

sheet
metal

dry laid cobbles

stove
part

beam
collapsed
framing material

4"x 3¾"beam

FEATURE 4

corrugated
metal

UNIT 5

concrete

UNIT 4

fallen
concrete post

collapsed
wall

flat
metal

cobbles and
concrete

corrugated metal
metal tank
(stove or sink?)

corrugated
metal

sheet metal

chicken
wire

4 pieces of
galvanized sheet
metal with roof
nail holes

buried
corrugated
metal

barbed wire,
chicken wire

window
screen

several
1"x 6" boards

Figure 7. Plan view of Features 2 and 4, the house remains.

On the northwest side of the porch slab was a 16-foot-long row of exposed dry-laid cobbles. Part of this alignment, which appeared to be in the form of a rectangle, was located by probing. The exact function of this alignment was unclear, but it may have served as a footing for the frame building once located here, or it may have been simply a row of cobbles placed along the edge of the building to prevent animals from getting under it. The presence of numerous 1-inch boards and 4 × 4-inch timbers indicated that a frame building had been located here, evidence supported by Figures 2 and 3. The 4 × 4-inch pieces appeared to have been roof beams. The roofs of both the porch and the frame room had been covered with roofing paper.

Excavation

Two 3-foot-square excavation units were placed in Feature 4. Unit 4 was excavated in one level in the fill on top of the concrete porch slab. This water-deposited sand fill was 7 inches in depth. All the artifactual material recovered was found in contact with the porch floor. Unit 5, excavated on the northwest side of the porch slab within the area enclosed by the cobble rectangle, was dug in three levels to a depth of 10 inches below the surface, where sterile soil was encountered. The upper 7 inches of fill was sand containing artifacts. It lay on a 3-inch layer of ash, charcoal, and artifacts.

Artifacts

Excavation Units 4 and 5 both produced artifacts. In Unit 4, 13 artifacts, representing a minimum of 13 individual objects, all but one of which were metal, were recovered. These artifacts were three 8d wire nails, two 7/8-inch roofing nails, two 1 1/2-inch roofing nails, an iron washer, a bolt, part of a horse-harness tug chain, a valve stem cap from an automobile tire that appeared to be of recent origin, and a piece of a possible gas (butane?) refrigerator. The nonmetal artifact was a piece of hard rubber or plastic from an unidentifiable object.

Excavation Unit 5 produced 175 whole and fragmentary artifacts representing a minimum of 137 objects from three levels (Figure 8). Food-related artifacts included a food jar, an evaporated milk can, a "HERSHEY'S COCOA" can lid, a metal fruit-jar-lid liner (all from Level 1), and a food jar from Level 2. The latter jar, which may have been part of the assemblage from Level 1, had been manufactured by the Hazel-Atlas Glass Company, 1920 to 1964 (Toulouse 1971:239). The evaporated milk can measured 207 by 207 and was of a type that, according to Simonis (n.d., n.p.), dated to 1931 to 1948.

Artifacts related to food preparation and consumption activities were an unknown porcelain form from Level 1 and a hardpaste white earthenware, decal-decorated saucer, two other unidentifiable ceramic forms, and an unidentifiable light green depression-glass object from Level 2. None of these were specifically datable, although the depression glass dated to after about 1925.

Leisure and recreation artifacts included .22-short cartridge cases, one with a "U" headstamp from Level 1, and a .22 Winchester Rimfire (WRF) or Remington Special, dating from 1890 to the present (Barnes 1972:275). Level 2 revealed a fragment of a phonograph record, and Level 3 contained a child's toy jack from a ball and jack set.

Medical and health-related artifacts were two foil tubes, one each from Levels 1 and 2. These had once contained salve or other ointment. The tube from Level 2 retained its phenolic screw cap.

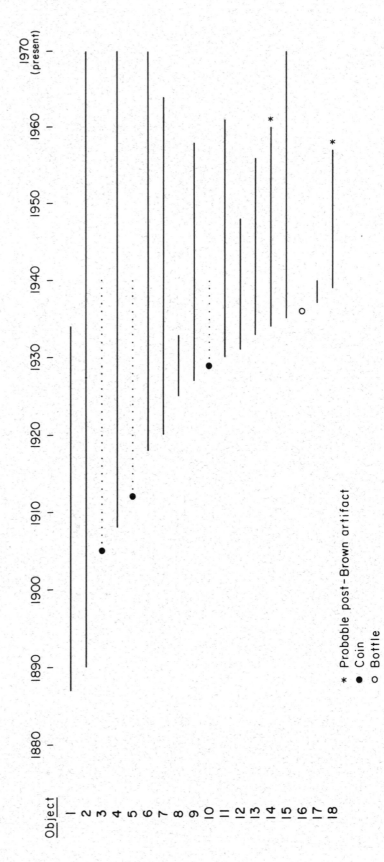

Figure 8. Brown homestead, composite artifact dates.

OBJECT	MARK OR DATABLE FORM	DATE
1. shotgun shell	"PETERS/VICTOR"	1887–1934
2. cartridge	.22 Winchester Rimfire (WRF) or Remington Special	1890–Present
3. coin	dime	1905
4. can	oval tobacco can	1908–Present
5. coin	nickel	1912
6. bottle	Schilling's spices	1918–Present
7. bottle	Hazel-Atlas Glass Co.	1920–1964
8. ceramic object	"ELPCO"	ca. 1925–1933
9. insulator	Porcelain Products, Inc.	1927–1958
10. coin	penny	1929
11. bottle	Maywood Glass Co.	1930–1961
12. can	evaporated milk can	1931–1948
13. bottle	Glass Container Corp.	1933–1956
14. shotgun shell	"REM-PET"	1934–1960
15. can and key	beer can; can key ("church key")	1935–Present
16. bottle	Owens-Illinois Glass Co.	1936
17. token	Arizona tax token	1937–1940
18. bottle	Latchford-Marble Glass Co.	1939–1957

Figure 8. Brown homestead, composite artifact dates, continued.

Level 2 artifacts that had a personal association were a shoe fragment, a snap from female clothing, a man's clothing button, two shell buttons (one with two and the other with four holes), and a tooth from a yellow plastic (?) comb. A tooth from a hard-rubber comb came from Level 3.

Tools and hardware-related artifacts were one machine bolt, one washer, two hexagonal nuts, two pieces of iron wire, a 5/8-inch staple, 27 galvanized roofing nails ranging in length from 7/8 to 1 1/2 inch, 20 wire nails from 8d to 16d in size, and six nails that were either fragments or unidentifiable nails. Level 2 artifacts in this functional category were one file, one bolt, one slotted clinch rivet, four different pieces of wire, nine roofing nails 7/8 to 1 1/2 inches in length, 11 wire nails ranging in size from 4d to 12d, and four nails that were either fragments or unidentified.

Artifacts associated with communication were limited to two fountain-pen parts from Level 1. A pen point had "IRIDIUM [in script]/TIPPED/U.S.A." on it. The other pen part was a plastic or hard-rubber piece on which the pen point rested.

Miscellaneous artifacts from Level 1 were a 1905 Barber-head dime and a 1929 Lincoln penny. Level 2 produced a metal lid for an unidentified container, a safety pin, a 1912 V nickel, an Arizona tax token, and a small prehistoric lithic flake. The tax token dated to 1937 to 1940 (Wagner 1973:365).

Thirty-six fragments representing a minimum of 13 objects were classified as totally unidentified. These included artifacts made of glass, ceramic, metal, and other materials whose size or condition precluded identification of function, form, content, or specific use.

Faunal Analysis

Levels 2 and 3 contained a total of 15 faunal remains (Strand 1990). Level 2 produced a humerus, a phalanx, and a rib, probably from one or more domestic goats that were known to have been raised by the Brown family. These bones could not be identified more precisely than the order Artiodactyla. This level also had a humerus and ulna of a domestic chicken (*Gallus gallus*) and a wing bone of a possible Gambel's quail (*Lophortyx* cf. *gambelii*). Two additional fragments of bone were unidentifiable. Level 3 produced seven burned bone fragments that were unidentifiable.

FEATURE 5 (ROCK WALL)

Feature 5 was a low, dry-laid rock wall, two courses high, running along the foot of the terrace from a point just north of Feature 2 south almost to Feature 6, approximately 80 feet. There was a 2-foot break in this wall at the northwest corner of Feature 2. The remnant of a 1 × 4-inch post was located on one side of this opening.

FEATURE 6, EXCAVATION UNIT 2

Feature Description

The dugout, Feature 6, was an L-shaped pit excavated by Brown into the terrace slope. Only the front part of it was lined with a low, dry-laid rock wall. The front part of the structure was 8 feet 3 inches wide, and it extended into the terrace slope 11 feet 3 inches, where it widened to 15 feet 8 inches. Excavation of the dugout extended a total of 24 feet 3 inches into the terrace. The feature was intended to be a root cellar but had never been completed.

Excavation

A 3-foot-square unit was excavated in the eastern portion of the feature to a depth of 12 inches below the present ground surface (PGS). Many artifacts were recovered in the sand and gravel matrix, but the unit was terminated after reaching a layer of caliche and cobbles.

Artifacts

The surface and Excavation Unit 2, combined, produced 17 fragments representing a minimum of five artifacts. A "turned pink" machine-made quart milk bottle (1920 to 1940) was the only artifact collected from the surface.

Excavation Unit 2 contained 11 fragments of a straw-colored food jar (1920 to 1940) made by the Hazel-Atlas Glass Company, 1920 to 1964 (Toulouse 1971:239). Four more glass fragments were from two bottles, the original contents of which remained unknown. One of these bottles was "turned pink" in color (1920 to 1940) and was made by the Maywood Glass Company, 1930 to 1961 (Toulouse 1971:357). A metal threaded lid for a food jar also was recovered from this excavation.

Faunal Analysis

A fifth metatarsal, possibly from a kit fox (cf. *Vulpes macrotis*), was collected from Level 1 of Excavation Unit 2 (Strand 1990).

FEATURE 7 (TRASH SCATTER)

Feature Description

This artifact scatter, located on the western edge of the site at the foot of the terrace, measured approximately 90 feet east-west by 25 feet north-south.

Artifacts

On its surface Feature 7 had nine artifacts representing nine individual objects: a threaded metal food-jar lid, an evaporated milk can measuring 214 by 415, a coffee-can end, a machine-made food can, a frying pan handle embossed "PATENTED ACME," a piece of a thin sheet-steel stove, an all-steel, "church-key" opened beer can, and an all-steel, cone-top beer can. The two beer cans and the "church key" all dated to after 1935.

Noted but not collected at Feature 7 were pieces of poultry netting, hog wire, and barbed wire, part of the thin sheet-steel stove mentioned above, a "HILLS BROS." coffee can, several cone-top and regular all-steel beer cans, an automobile muffler, a top hoop from a wooden nail key, the head end of a metal bed frame, a windmill fan blade, automobile seat springs, and a partially buried 50-gallon drum.

FEATURE 8 (STOCK TANK)

This feature was a concrete-lined stock tank 14 1/2 feet in diameter and 24 inches deep. The interior of this tank was plastered with a sandy mix of concrete over cobbles. A 10-foot length of 3-inch diameter galvanized pipe protruded from the west side of this feature. Part of the pipe was buried under sand; only its ends were exposed. Both ends of this pipe were threaded, suggesting it may have been salvaged from somewhere else and reused on the water tank. Numerous 1960s-to-1970s cans and bottles were found in this feature. Because of their recent origin, none were collected or analyzed.

FEATURE 9 (WELL)

The well was situated just east of Feature 8 and consisted of a depression, and five wooden posts. The depression, which had a 3/4-inch-diameter iron pipe protruding from its center, was about 5 feet deep and 15 feet in diameter. The backdirt from the excavation of the well lay on the east and south sides of the depression. Only the fan and its tail remained of the windmill; the tower had been removed from the site.

On the north side of the well depression were four mesquite posts, 5 to 6 inches in diameter, vertically placed. All were round, but at least one had been roughly squared. These posts, situated in a rectangular pattern (2 1/2 × 6 feet), may have been part of the support for a motor used to pump water. The posts had all been notched on their inside edges to create a ledge that probably supported a floor or base on which the motor rested. They also had large steel bolts in them.

FEATURE 10 (COBBLE ALIGNMENT)

Feature 10 consisted of a cobble alignment and a wire fence. The alignment ran alongside the wash to the east of the site and was used to divert water away from the windmill. The fence was made of sections of hog wire, poultry netting, and barbed wire.

SITE DATING

The artifacts from the site generally reflected the years 1933 to 1939, when the Brown family lived at the homestead (Figure 8). A few items, which may have been deposited by prospectors in the 1950s, seemed to postdate the Browns. The artifacts found in the stock tank obviously postdated the Brown occupation of the site.

INTERPRETATION

As outlined in the Introduction, there were three research topics thought relevant to address with Brown homestead site data. These focused on subsistence and food behavior, on sociocultural interaction, and on vernacular architecture. Data to evaluate these topics were derived from three sources: the archaeological mapping and the artifacts collected from the surface and excavations, the historical documentation, and, finally, the interviews conducted with informants possessing firsthand information about the site.

SUBSISTENCE AND FOOD BEHAVIOR

Information relating to food, derived from all these source, made it clear that the Brown family had relied primarily on store purchases, their garden, their domesticated animals, and on hunting to satisfy their subsistence needs.

It is likely that the majority of the cash earned by the family from the sale of firewood, trapping, selling of reptiles, and other sources went for the purchase of food, although investigators acquired no hard data with which to support this assertion. Another area of major expense would have been fuel and upkeep for the Browns' vehicles (truck and automobile) and the motor they used to saw up the firewood. The Browns used the cash obtained from the sale of firewood in Phoenix to buy groceries there. They appeared to have purchased few groceries in the closer, smaller, and probably more expensive communities of New River or Black Canyon City.

The relationship between purchased food and food produced on the homestead can be discussed only in a general manner because no available documentation allows for us to quantify either category. The artifacts collected from the surface and the excavations at the site and the food-related information recalled by the informants provide all we know about the subject. In many cases the artifacts collected, such as bottles, jars, and cans, could be identified only as general food containers because their specific original contents could not be determined. Although a few of these artifacts may have postdated the Brown residence on the site, most appeared to have been contemporaneous. Investigators did identify more specific food products, which are listed above with the artifact descriptions: a small juice can, evaporated milk cans, a coffee can, a Hershey's cocoa can lid, a Karo syrup bottle, a Schilling's spice bottle, and a milk bottle. Given the lack of refrigeration, the purchase of evaporated milk was undoubtedly more common than that of fresh milk. Other food items found archaeologically were a fruit pit (probably peach) and beef, chicken, goat, and quail bones. Home canning of garden produce occurred on the site and was reflected by a fruit jar lid liner and remnants of a Mason jar located during the 1987 survey at Feature 3.

The senior author elicited from the informants a list of food items, other than those enumerated above, that were purchased from grocery stores, but this in no way reflects a complete inventory. Many of the items named generally produce no archaeological remains, especially those packaged in cardboard boxes or cloth sacks or simply wrapped in paper. The informants recalled eating raisins, flour, beef, bacon, sugar, oatmeal, beans, and wheat at the Brown homestead.

The family's garden provided a variety of food items and was a major source of food. The relatively long growing season enabled the Browns to maintain a garden for most of the year. Among other vegetables, they grew tomatoes, corn, squash, green beans, and peppers, as well as peanuts, which did well in the sandy soil. The citrus trees that the Browns expected to provide food and, possibly, fruit for sale proved to be unviable, partly because of natural events and partly because of the goats.

In addition to goats and chickens, the remains of which are mentioned above, the Browns also ate pigs and chicken eggs. The goats provided milk that was used for drinking, for cooking, and for making cheese.

The Browns apparently made limited use of the wild resources available to them. Archaeological field work did not locate any rabbit, deer, or fish remains. Informants reported that only one deer had been killed and eaten, but cottontail rabbits had often been shot for food. JD and Carroll had walked downriver to Lake Pleasant to fish, but how often they had gone fishing, given the distance, could not be ascertained. The Browns exploited wild plant foods only on occasion. Informants mentioned mesquite beans, jojoba beans, and prickly pear in this regard. The family collected, ground up, and baked jojoba beans in fudge. They made prickly pear fruit into jelly, and on one occasion after several days of high river water, which precluded them from bringing groceries to the site, they cooked and ate prickly pear pads.

The homesteaders had difficulty preserving food; meat, fresh milk, and other perishables brought to the site had a short shelf life before they spoiled. The Brown family employed a number of strategies to help preserve food, including some canning of garden produce, making jerky and smoking of fresh meat, and using a "desert cooler." In addition, the family reportedly had an electrical refrigerator at one point but used it probably for a very short time. The Browns could have made both store-purchased meat and that obtained from butchering pigs and goats into jerky or, alternatively, could have smoked the meat over mesquite wood chips above the pit created by the excavation of adobe used to make bricks for construction of part of the house. The desert cooler provided, through evaporation, a means to keep food relatively cool, but it would not preserve food for long. This device, constructed in varying forms, was a common homestead feature during the 1930s and earlier.

In summary, it can be said that the Brown family enjoyed an eclectic diet that was usually varied and well balanced. Only rarely was food in short supply either because of a lack of money or because the vagaries of the Agua Fria River prevented access to the outside world for extended periods of time.

In regard to the question of which was more important on a homestead, the amount of land cultivated or the ability to irrigate, little can be said. Obviously, successful cultivation could not exist without water in the area of Arizona homesteaded by Charles Brown. Brown was able to irrigate using his windmill to pump water, but his irrigation system was simple in form and limited in size. The cultivation of a garden, made possible through irrigation, enabled the family to have fresh food that otherwise would have been unavailable to them, and it helped ensure a more stable existence at the homestead. Finally, and more to the point, the National Homestead Act of 1862 mandated cultivation. Without making at least a token effort at it, Brown never would have received a patent for his land.

SOCIOCULTURAL INTERACTION

The Brown family's network of relationships with the world outside their homestead took many forms, but it can be said that they tended to be directed inward rather than outward in their daily activities. In fact, Bobbie Murray, who lived on the homestead during part of her early childhood, thought that the family had not been particularly outgoing and that socializing with neighbors had not been an important part of their homestead life. Other informants supported this assessment. Although these generalizations may be true, the Brown family's life on the homestead and their socializing actually had been a complex situation about which it was difficult to elicit information. Various members of the family engaged in socializing activities at different levels and degrees of intensity. The two oldest daughters, Jettie and Oneta, who did not live on the homestead in 1933, but who spent considerable periods of time there until 1939, certainly led lives different from the rest of the Brown children or their parents. Both these women married about 1931, and both had daughters who spent much of their time on the homestead. The younger Brown children had less freedom to leave the homestead than the adults and probably had little reason to do so.

Other than Brown's seeming personal predilection for isolation, the family had more concrete reasons for its limited contact with the outside world. The remoteness of the site necessarily meant that access would be a problem. The Browns had to travel from Phoenix to the homestead on simple, unpaved dirt roads, which beyond the Gingery Ranch deteriorated into simple tracks in the riverbed. Frequent flooding of the Agua Fria River and Gingery's intractability exacerbated the access problem both for the family and for visitors from the outside. On every trip in or out of the homestead the family faced the constant threat of getting an automobile stuck in the sand or mud. Of course, four-wheel drive vehicles, which would have lessened the problem, were unavailable in the 1930s. To make matters worse, the Browns could often only afford used cars that would occasionally break down and were sometimes abandoned, as the vehicle remains at the homestead attest. Flat tires were also a frequent annoyance.

These factors not only complicated socializing activities but inhibited to some degree the Browns' ability to get their firewood and other products to the Phoenix market. Today, when a trip from Phoenix to the Brown homestead requires a little over one hour, it is difficult to appreciate that the trip took Brown the better part of a day to accomplish.

The Browns enjoyed the homestead and being by themselves. Family members provided much of their own recreation and spent much of their time socializing among themselves. The boys, JD and Carroll, spent time wandering around the countryside exploring, hunting, and trapping. The river offered a place for the children to play because permanent water surfaced at the Brown homestead. The granddaughters played with paper dolls, and all the children went barefoot. All in all, outdoor activities were the rule rather than the exception at the Brown homestead. Music was a part of the Browns' life. They had a phonograph player, and JD played the guitar while the others joined in by singing. The family often spent evenings outdoors singing and listening to music. Another form of recreation the informants mentioned was card playing. Betting with Arizona tax tokens that were worth one mill, or a tenth of a cent, the adults played poker, which they jokingly called "mill-ante" poker.

Within a two- or three-mile stretch of the Agua Fria River lay seven homesteads, ranches, or squatter locations (Figure 1). From south to north they belonged to Tyler, Brown, Avis, Prawl, an unknown squatter (?) named Tommy, Gingery, and Decker (Ayres 1988:11). The next nearest neighbors were several miles distant. It would be reasonable to expect that given the remoteness of the homestead and the transportation problem, the homesteaders would have socialized extensively among themselves. Such does not appear to have been the case, although the informants may not have recalled many casual or irregular encounters.

Their nearest neighbors were the people with whom the Browns should have had the most frequent contact. Brown's oldest daughter occupied the Tyler homestead for about one year, and Jettie spent as much time at the Browns' as she did on her own homestead. The family maintained substantially less contact with the Avis family, the Browns' nearest neighbors. Neighborly activities included the Avis children playing with Browns' granddaughters, the Avises eating at least one meal at the Browns' place, Frank Avis helping Charles Brown in an attempt to locate his property corners, the Browns frequently borrowing tools from Avis, and the gift of one or more pigs from Avis to the Browns, including Jettie. On one or more occasions members of the Avis family joined the Browns in an evening of music and singing outdoors. Undoubtedly the two families had many other contacts.

How much contact occurred between Prawl and the Browns remained unclear, but at least Carroll Brown was well acquainted with Prawl. Contact with Decker was probably limited to casual conversation at the times the Browns had to past through his homestead on their way into and out of the river bed. Tommy was only vaguely remembered by the Avises, and the Browns did not mention him.

The rancher Gingery (Ayres 1988:17) was a special case. Homesteader contact with him was generally a very negative experience. His refusal to allow them access to their homesteads across his land ultimately led to physical violence that resulted in Frank Avis injuring a hand and Charles Brown being arrested. Avis in fact had more problems with Gingery than did Brown (Ayres 1988:26). A subsequent court case resolved the issue by granting the homesteaders access to their properties. Exactly why Gingery was so hostile towards homesteaders is not known, but the fact that they were removing federal and, in Brown's case, federal and state lands from Gingery's use may have generated the enmity. Up to the time the homesteaders arrived, Gingery may have enjoyed free and illegal use of these lands for grazing purposes. Except in the case of Gingery, there was little or no open hostility among the residents of the area. Gingery left the ranch in the mid 1940s; where he went remains unknown.

No evidence from informants, or other sources, indicated that the homesteaders had ever engaged in labor exchanges of any kind. Brown could tap plenty of labor within his own family, including his sons-in-law. Avis, a very self-sufficient and independent individual, did not generally rely on outside help. However, on a few occasions he may have paid one of the Brown boys to work for him on a limited basis.

The Browns' activities beyond the confines of the Agua Fria River were even less clear. Informants were not certain what social activities Brown engaged in while in Phoenix, for example. Visiting relatives may have been the major form of socializing. Charles's brother Walter lived in Phoenix. Ora Lee's family lived in Prescott, and the Browns visited her relatives there, although probably less frequently than Charles's relatives. During the homestead years, the family went no farther than Phoenix and Prescott, although daughter Jettie had spent some time in California prior to filing on the Tyler homestead. Other than socializing with relatives, the Browns made several other contacts with the outside world: they had frequent contact with nonrelatives when they sold firewood, snakes, Gila monsters, and furs or bought groceries, gasoline, and other supplies in Phoenix or sold pork to miners in Mayer.

The oldest daughters, at least, attended dances in New River and Black Canyon City, most frequently in the one-room schoolhouse at Black Canyon City. The dances were attended by cowboys, homesteaders, and others; liquor was usually present, and fighting by some of the men was almost guaranteed.

For the younger children the only outside contact of any real consequence came when they attended school in Black Canyon City or New River. During the time they were in school they lived in Black Canyon City at the Kay Copper Mine. Ora Lee and the younger children had visited the homestead on weekends, but Ayres did not ascertain how frequently they had done so.

Relatives and friends from the outside did not often visit the homestead, primarily because of the distance to travel and the vagaries of the Agua Fria River. An exception to this was the visits by prospectors who roamed the hills along the Agua Fria River throughout the Great Depression. These men often stopped at the Brown homestead. One hauled ore via burro from the Tip Top Mine through the area, one lived a few miles away, and some were more or less transients. Undoubtedly the attractive Brown women provided at least part of the reason for their presence.

Although Brown had been an avid Baptist in his youth, church did not play a role in his life or that of his family, or for that matter in the lives of the others residing along the river.

For the most part the Brown family's contacts with their neighbors and the outside world seemed to have been brief and sporadic. They apparently developed few lasting personal relationships over the years, and when they left their homestead in 1939 they had few ties to sever.

VERNACULAR ARCHITECTURE

The only building at the Brown homestead of any consequence was the house (Features 2 and 4). Details of its appearance in 1990, the spatial relationship of it to the other buildings and structures on the site, measurements, and information about its internal space area are all discussed above in as much detail as is available (Figures 6 and 9).

As was the case with the Avis homestead, the Browns built a simple, crude, one-room temporary residence until they could construct a more substantial dwelling. This developmental sequence was also reported for the Wintersburg homesteaders (Stein 1981:9). The first Brown house was made from lumber and corrugated metal sheets taken from a building at the Kay Copper Mine near Black Canyon City. During a violent windstorm, the house was severely damaged, and it washed away in the flood that followed. Informants believed that the second, and last, house had been built sometime in 1934. The material salvaged from the first house had been used to build the chicken house.

The second house consisted of three parts: a porch, a large wood frame room, and a small adobe room. The informants could not recall the sequence of construction, but subsurface excavation revealed several clues to the sequence of building at the Brown homestead. The interior plaster of Feature 2 overlapped the concrete slab, indicating that the interior had been covered after the slab had been poured. The consistency of the concrete in the foundation of Feature 4 and the slab of the adobe (Feature 2) suggested they may have been poured at the same time. Wooden forms had been used on the interior, and cobble acted as a form on the exterior of the foundation. A seam in the concrete between the porch's floor and the building's foundation suggested that the porch had been poured later. Surrounding the house had been an ocotillo fence probably intended to keep the goats away from the house.

The house, oriented northwest-southeast, had the porch and entry on the southeast side. The open-sided porch had a concrete floor 7 × 13 feet in size. Surrounding the slab was a low cobble and cement wall. The concrete slab appeared to have been poured after the walls had been built. The wooden porch roof supports and other exposed wood had been painted white at one time. The porch roof had sloped to the southeast and had been covered with roofing paper.

The porch had been attached to the southeast side of a large (approximately 16 × 17 feet overall) wood-frame, gable-roofed room, the roof of which had been covered with roofing paper. On its southwest side, at least, the gable end may have had as much as a 2-foot overhang. The exterior wall covering had consisted of boards 10 or 12 inches wide and 1 inch thick, vertically placed. Whether the interior had been finished was not ascertained. This room, which once had a wooden floor, may have rested directly on the ground. There was a row of dry laid river cobbles where the southwest wall of this room would have been, but whether this alignment had served as part of a foundation or had been simply a row of cobbles placed along the base of the wall to keep animals from crawling under it could not be determined.

Figure 9. The house as it existed in 1990.

Behind the wood frame room was a small adobe room abutted against its northwest corner. This room, the last part of the house to be constructed, had been built of adobe bricks made on-site by Brown. It had a concrete floor, and its interior had been about 6 × 10 feet in size, although accurate measurements were not made because of the melted adobe present. This room had been used as the children's bedroom, but its size suggested that some of them might have slept elsewhere. Certainly in the summertime, some of the family had slept outdoors under one of the large mesquite trees surrounding the house, as was typical in the region (Jettie North). The walls of the interior of the adobe room had been covered with poultry netting and cement plaster. As can be seen above, the house had been a combination of purchased, probably scavenged, and locally available materials, including dimensioned lumber, cement, river cobbles, roofing paper, and adobe. The surface on and around Features 2 and 4, plus the three excavations in those features, produced examples of all these materials, in addition to window screen from Feature 2 and common and roofing nails from Feature 4. An electrical insulator found in Feature 3 may have been part of the electrical wiring system needed to provide electricity to the house from the Delco plant.

There had been nothing unique or special about the Brown house, and its homemade character was readily apparent. The house exhibited no special adaptive features to ameliorate the desert heat as were found at Wintersburg and elsewhere in Arizona (Sargeant 1960 as cited by Stein 1981:97; Young 1983 as cited by Stein 1988:82). Life at the Brown homestead probably had been somewhat comfortable because it was located near the river, which would have provided cool breezes, especially in the evenings.

The materials used to construct the Brown house were all commonly used at homesteads elsewhere. At Wintersburg, for example, wood frame and adobe houses were noted (Stein 1981:9). Not much is known about the homes of the Browns' immediate neighbors. The Tyler homestead had a two-room, 14 × 20-foot frame house, and the Avis house was of poured concrete. The size of the latter is unknown, but it clearly was the most substantial of all the homesteaders' houses along the Agua Fria in the 1930s. The original house at the Gingery Ranch was of adobe, and a later one was a wood-frame building (Ayres 1988:17). Based on the architecture alone, the Avis house seemed to reflect an attitude of greater permanency on the part of the homesteader as compared to the houses at the other homesteads.

5
SUMMARY AND CONCLUSIONS

The Brown homestead, located on the north side of the Agua Fria River in SW 1/4, sec. 12, T. 7N, R. 1E, Yavapai County, Arizona, was occupied from 1933 to 1939 by Charles J. Brown and his family. Earlier, the only homestead in the immediate area had been that of George W. Cavness who had filed on 160 acres around what later became the NO Ranch buildings. He filed on the property in 1912 and received a patent in 1915. Cavness promptly sold the homestead to C. A. Gingery, who occupied it until about the mid 1940s (Ayres 1988:17). In 1933 when Brown moved to the property, other homesteaders had already settled in the area or were about to settle there. The Avis family had established their homestead across the river to the southeast, Art Prawl had his between the Browns and the NO Ranch, and the Tylers (actually Jettie Brown Tyler) homesteaded about a mile downstream from Brown. The Avis, Prawl, and Tyler homesteads were the standard 160-acre parcels filed on under the rules of the National Homestead Act of 1862, as amended. Brown was the last of the three to receive a patent: it was not until after he had left the property that Brown filed a homestead entry form and his final proof, and he was subsequently issued a patent for the parcel in 1942. All three of these families had been living in Arizona before they settled on their homesteads. Researchers located no information relevant to Prawl's property.

Somewhat farther afield was the N. Bross Decker homestead a few miles north of the Gingery ranch, which was patented in 1942 about a month before Brown received his patent. Decker does not figure in this history of the study area except that his homestead was situated on the first crossing of the Agua Fria River as one went west from the Phoenix–Black Canyon City highway (Ayres 1988:27).

Of all the homesteaders along this part of the Agua Fria River, only Decker did not sell out to the Bard Cattle Company. Brown and Jettie Brown Tyler sold their homesteads to the Bard Cattle Company about 1943 or 1944. Gingery sold his interest to them about the same time (Ayres 1988:17). Avis, who sold Bard only his land on the north side of the river, continued to reside on his homestead on the south side of the river until he reached retirement age in the early 1960s (Bob Gilbreath). Avis ultimately replaced the land he sold to Bard with a parcel of a similar size on the south side of the river. Excluding the Cavness homestead, which is part of a thriving ranch today, Avis's place was by far the most successful homesteading effort of any in the area. The major reason for the longevity of both the Avis homestead and the ranch was probably the fact that an efficient system for irrigating fields had been constructed at both. Since the mid 1980s the Avis homestead has been abandoned. Because the property was determined not to be eligible for inclusion on the National Register of Historic Places, all the buildings and structures were removed by the Bureau of Reclamation as part of the process of clearing areas that will be inundated by the new Waddell Dam reservoir. After nearly 100 years of local settlement, only the ranch, now known as the Boulder Creek Ranch, still exists.

The events motivating the homesteaders to settle where they did along the Agua Fria River undoubtedly varied for each, but a major factor for most was the Great Depression, which created a situation of no jobs, and thus no money, in the cities. Although homesteading was never a panacea for these problems, it nonetheless provided a means for many in Arizona to reduce their living costs by acquiring a relatively free place to live.

Homesteading as a federally sanctioned activity began to decline in importance as a means to acquire land in Arizona by the late 1930s. Most of the land available during the 1930s was marginal in every respect, and most homesteaders undoubtedly were aware of this fact. Nevertheless, many unskilled individuals opted to settle on marginally productive land where they had some available water, could raise some food, could keep their initial expenses relatively low, and could eke out a subsistence-level livelihood.

Charles Brown typified many homesteaders of the 1930s because he was bankrupt and had no possibility of finding a job in Phoenix adequate to feed his wife and family of six children. The move to a homestead was his last resort. For Brown, as for many others, farming alone did not provide enough food or income on which to raise a family. Most homesteaders, like the Browns, had to generate income either through outside work or, for example, by cutting firewood. Both the Avis parents worked off their homestead on occasion. They worked for Bard at the NO or at another of his ranches from time to time. Frank Avis also drove a school bus (Doris Avis; Zona Gilbreath). Brown apparently did not work off his homestead. His small income came from the sale of mesquite firewood and occasionally from the sale of pork to miners. His oldest son also earned money for the family by trapping and selling furs and animals. Brown's oldest daughter may have contributed to the family's economic well-being from time to time as well. At the very least she contributed her labor to help make the Brown homestead a success. Typically, a homesteading woman would have been responsible for caring for young children, housework, and outdoor tasks such as gardening.

Stein (1981:93) reported that at Wintersburg nearly 66% of the homesteaders sold their land within six years of the issue date of the patent. Brown and his neighbors matched that figure to some extent. Charles Brown sold his property in less than two years (actually five years after he had left it), Jettie Brown Tyler sold hers in seven years, and Frank Avis sold his grazing land north of the river within five years after receiving the patent. Speculation, which is cited by Stein (1981:100) as the motivation of many of the Wintersburg homesteaders, does not appear to have been important for the Harquahala homesteaders also reported by Stein (1988:86).

Ayres found no evidence indicating that crass speculation had motivated the founding of Brown's homestead or those of his Agua Fria neighbors. These homesteads appeared to have been at first a refuge from unemployment and economic stress and only later became a potential source of capital. Speculation on a fast sale assumes a ready buyer, but there were no buyers on the Agua Fria until Bard began the expansion of his grazing lands in the mid 1940s. Thus, selling may have been opportunistic rather than planned, even for Brown, who kept his homestead for less than two years after he received the patent. He had after all spent nearly six hard years on his place, left to find work in California, and only then formally filed on it. Certainly the commitment by Avis and Cavness of money and labor to developing and maintaining irrigation systems suggested their intent from the outset to stay on the land.

Ten features were noted at the Brown homestead (the remains of a house in two parts, a privy, a dugout, a well, a stock tank, a rock alignment, a rock retaining wall, and two trash disposal areas) that had been built by Brown and his family and apparently had never been deliberately modified or changed over the years. Although itinerant prospectors occasionally used the house as late as the 1950s, nothing had been done to it since its abandonment in 1939. Additional features, for which few or no remains could be found, were noted on the homestead forms obtained from the Bureau of Land Management or through informants. These features included a goat corral, a fenced garden, an ocotillo fence around the house, a chicken house, a meat smoking pit, and a "desert cooler."

In addition to surface collection of artifacts, small excavations were performed in four features—the privy, the house, the adobe part of the house, and the dugout. Also, 21 pieces of fauna representing a minimum of seven individual animals were collected from the excavations. Identifiable animals were raccoon (of recent origin) and probably goat from Feature 1; cattle from Feature 2; goat, chicken, and Gambel's quail from Feature 4; and kit fox from Feature 6.

A total of 337 whole and fragmentary artifacts representing 239 individual items were collected from the surface and the excavations. Many of these, although classified as tools and hardware items, actually had an architectural use. Indeed, 26% of the artifacts were related to architecture; most of these came from Features 2 and 4, including nails, roofing paper, window screen, and an electrical insulator. Most of the box and common wire nails were of the sizes 6d to 16d commonly used to construct small wood-frame buildings.

Few automobile-related artifacts were collected, but parts of one or more automobiles were found on the site: a headlight lens from Feature 2, body parts at Feature 1 and southeast of Feature 4, a gas tank east of Feature 6, a muffler and car-seat springs at Feature 7, and a muffler and tail pipe south of the windmill and well.

The household furnishings found suggested that the family may have left some of these behind when they abandoned the homestead in 1939. These included parts of a cast-iron stove at Features 3 and 4 and most of a stamped sheet-steel stove at Feature 7. Part of a possible refrigerator or other appliance came from Feature 4, and a bed spring (between Features 6 and 7) and part of a bed frame (Feature 7) were also found.

Surprisingly, artifacts that unambiguously related to women and children were few in number. The only toy found was a lone jack from a ball and jack game in Feature 4. Other children's artifacts were shoe fragments from Features 1 and 2. A woman's or girl's leather belt with an iron buckle came from Feature 1, and a snap from female clothing was found at Feature 4.

Male-oriented artifacts were more numerous, even though fewer males had occupied the site. Males were present in 1933 and after 1936, when female presence was limited or nonexistent. Male-oriented artifacts included shoes, clothing parts, a tobacco can, a dry-snuff bottle, and alcoholic-beverage bottles. Although both men and women used tobacco and drank alcoholic beverages during the Depression era, it is more likely that in this case these artifacts were male related, as was generally the case for the period.

All in all, the artifacts from the homestead reflected domestic activities that would be expected at a rural residence. The quantity and range of functions represented were limited, which may reflect the fact that silting had covered much of the trash at the site. It may also be related to the fact that the homestead had been occupied during the Great Depression when little money was available with which to purchase manufactured goods.

The Brown family, like many others in Arizona, chose homesteading as the solution to the economic problems brought about by the Great Depression. For them the homestead provided a refuge of last resort, a relatively free place to live and to raise food, a way to earn a modest income, and a base from which the children could develop into responsible and productive individuals. Today the Brown family members are scattered across three states: California, Arizona, and Colorado. All lead successful lives, some at least are well off financially, and many are well traveled.

The children in retrospect viewed their life on the homestead as very positive. Jettie said that being able to homestead during the Depression had helped economically disadvantaged people maintain their self-respect during the hard times. Although physically taxing, homesteading had been rewarding work. On the relatively isolated homestead one became part of nature, acquired the freedom to explore the out-of-doors, and experienced an enduring feeling of family togetherness and companionship. That they all remembered homesteading with good feelings is evidenced by the fact that they have often returned to visit the site and to reminisce about their life there.

The story of the Brown family living in their isolated homestead environment along the Agua Fria River in the 1930s has many of the elements of a Zane Grey western novel. In their intra- and interpersonal relationships we glimpse (albeit sometimes only implicitly in this paper) love, hate, friendship, personal problems, economic challenges, conflict between a hateful rancher and the homesteaders, and ultimate family success.

SOURCES

PRIMARY SOURCES

Most of the primary homestead records relevant to the history of the Brown homestead are completed General Land Office forms. These are often difficult to cite in the traditional archaeological format. Therefore, to facilitate the use of these sources they are cited within the text as needed but are not listed in the References section. Brown was issued patent no. 1115272 dated November 11, 1942 (Serial 073800) for his homestead. Tyler was issued patent no.1090598 dated June 15, 1937 (Serial 073736). Likewise, information gleaned from informants is cited under their names in the text; they are not listed in the References section.

REFERENCES CITED

Ayres, James E.
   1988   Historic Homestead and Ranch Survey along the Middle Agua Fria River. In *Historical Archaeological Investigations at Dam Construction Camps in Central Arizona*, edited by A.E. Rogge and Cindy Meyers, pp. 9–47. Dames and Moore, Phoenix.

Ayres, James E., and Gregory R. Seymour
   1990   *Life on a 1930s Homestead: Historical Archaeological Investigations of the Brown Homestead on the Middle Agua Fria River, Yavapai County, Arizona.* SWCA, Inc., Environmental Consultants, Tucson.

Barnes, Frank C.
   1972   *Cartridges of the World.* Revised 4th ed. DBI Books, Northfield, Ill.

Brown, David E. (editor)
   1982   Biotic Communities of the American Southwest—United States and Mexico. *Desert Plants* 4(1–4).

Gates, William C., Jr., and Dana Ormerod
   1982   The East Liverpool Pottery District: Identification of Manufacturers and Marks. *Historical Archaeology* 16 (1–2).

Hull-Walski, Deborah A., and James E. Ayres
   1989   Laboratory Methods and Data Computerization. *The Historical Archaeology of Dam Construction Camps in Central Arizona*, Vol.3. Dames & Moore, Phoenix.

Lehner, Lois
   1988   *Lehners Encyclopedia of U.S. Marks on Pottery, Porcelain, and Clay.* Collector Books, Paducah, Ky.

Simonis, Donald E.
   n.d.   Condensed/Evaporated Milk Cans—Chronology for Dating Historical Sites. Ms. on file, Bureau of Land Management, Kingman, Ariz.

Stein, Pat H.
  1981   Wintersburg: An Archaeological, Archival, and Folk Account of Homesteading in Arizona. *The Palo Verde Archaeological Investigations*, Part 2. Museum of Northern Arizona Research Paper 21. Flagstaff.

  1988   *Homesteading in the Depression: A Study of Two Short-Lived Homesteads in the Harquahala Valley, Arizona.* Northland Research, Inc., Flagstaff.

Strand, Jennifer
  1990   Faunal Report for AZ T:4:55 (ASM). Ms. on file, SWCA, Inc., Tucson, Ariz.

Toulouse, Julian H.
  1971   *Bottle Makers and Their Marks.* Thomas Nelson, New York.

U.S. Department of the Interior, National Park Service
  1986   *Guidelines for Completing National Register of Historic Places Forms.* National Register Bulletin 16. U.S. Department of the Interior, National Park Service, Washington.

Wagner, J. R.
  1973   The Sales Tax Token 1937–1945. *The Numismatist.* March.

Zumwalt, Betty
  1980   *Ketchup, Pickles, Sauces—19th Century Food in Glass.* Mark West Pub., Fulton, Calif.